ALAN TITCHMARSH'S
AVANT-GARDENING

ALAN TITCHMARSH'S AVANT-GARDENING

A guide to
One-upmanship in the Garden

with drawings by
Keith Ratling

SOUVENIR
PRESS

ISBN 0 285 62657 4

Filmset in Monophoto Bembo by
Northumberland Press Ltd, Gateshead
Tyne and Wear
Printed and bound in Great Britain by
Richard Clay (The Chaucer Press) Ltd,
Bungay, Suffolk

Contents

Acknowledgements

My thanks to Peter Wood, Editor of *Amateur Gardening*, for giving me permission to reproduce material which first appeared in that magazine, and to Tessa Harrow of Souvenir Press for her encouragement and enthusiasm. To all my friends and colleagues in gardening (many of whom are mentioned in this book) I offer my thanks and, should they think it necessary, my apologies. Most of them are avant-gardeners to a man (or woman).

The Avant-Gardener

There's no escaping it; the garden is a hotbed of fashion. It's not enough to keep the lawn mown, to 'do the bedding out' and to kill off the greenfly. To keep up with the Lloyd-Joneses it's necessary for the most reluctant gardener to be aware of what is socially, horticulturally acceptable, and what is definitely beyond the pale.

It's not a matter of simple snobbery, nor a case of the most expensive being the best. It's a complicated combination of taste, fashion and art that instantly identifies itself as up-market gardening.

To excel at this horticultural one-upmanship the avant-gardener needs to know just what's 'in' and 'out'. Which flowers, fruits and vegetables are most highly prized? What should one wear? Which tools should one use, which names should one drop, which gardens should one visit, and which nurseries should one patronise? Then there's the social calendar to consider, the staff one should employ, the societies one should join and, most important of all, the language one should use.

This little book offers all the answers and will steer you clear of the pitfalls that will instantly brand your garden as infra dig rather than avant-garde.

Garden Talk

The greatest stumbling block for any aspiring avant-gardener is botanical nomenclature (those dreaded Latin names). With a strong enough air of confidence it is actually possible to get through life (or at least an afternoon in somebody's garden) without uttering a single generic, specific, varietal or cultivarietal name, but it's tricky.

There is, however, a compromise. It is generally understood that each plant has a Latin name which usually consists of two parts. For example, *Sorbus aucuparia* (the Latin name for the mountain ash). Keen gardeners, though, will never refer to it in the flesh by its full name. They'll simply say: 'That's a fine *aucuparia* over there.'

This technique is a godsend. Memorise only three of these 'specific epithets' (which can be applied to more than one plant) and you're in with a chance of being thought reasonably expert. I'd suggest:

1 *speciosa* (roughly translated it means 'lovely')
2 *superba* (even better)
3 *kewensis* (they're bound to have something bred at Kew)

When standing some distance from a group of plants, wave your arm loosely in the air and say: 'Hasn't *speciosa/superba/kewensis* been odd this year?' Your host is bound to have at least one plant within the panorama that boasts that name and you can relax for the rest of the day safe in the knowledge that when your host thinks about it, the plant will most certainly have been odd.

Should you feel rather more daring, then plump for a more descriptive appellation:

Wave your arm loosely in the air and say: 'Hasn't speciosa/superba/kewensis *been odd this year?'*

alba – for a plant with white flowers

lutea – for yellow flowers

rubra – for red flowers

caerulea – for blue flowers, but watch your pronunciation doesn't let you down (ky-*rue*-lee-a)

rosea – for pink flowers

nigra – for anything dark and dingy

If you're really lily-livered and want to know the name of a plant you're looking at, do not say, 'What's this?' Far better to say, 'Which one is this?' This implies that you are quite aware of the plant's genus but the nicety of the specific epithet escapes you at the moment. It does, however, leave you with the problem of guessing the genus once you've been told the species.

Name dropping

Dropping the odd plant name will stand you in good stead as far as expertise goes. Dropping the odd person's name will make you even more interesting (provided you drop the right people). The following are guaranteed to add an air of fashionable authority to your conversation:

Christopher Lloyd (1921–   ).   The Bernard Levin of the gardening world. Owner of Great Dixter, contributor to *Country Life* and proponent of the mixed border.

Vita Sackville-West (1892–1962).   Until her death the Virginia Woolf of the gardening world. Creator of Sissinghurst, wife (though the title is not one that suited her) of Harold Nicolson and originator of the craze for White Gardens.

Graham Stuart Thomas (1909–   ).   One-time gardens adviser to the National Trust. The man responsible for filling avant-gardens with old fashioned shrub roses.

Gertrude Jekyll (1843–1932).   Pronounced to rhyme with 'treacle'. High-priestess of garden colour-scheming. Worked well with the architect Sir Edwin Lutyens. Most large, old, landed-gentry gardens in Surrey were, it seems, designed by her (though there is something of the 'Queen Elizabeth I slept here' about this).

William Robinson (1838–1935).   Irishman. Leading light in the campaign against bedding out and a return to 'natural gardening'. Created superb bedding schemes at Gravetye Manor in Sussex.

Lancelot 'Capability' Brown (1716–1783).   Landscape architect who enjoyed ripping up the countryside and replanting it so that it looked more natural. Any old garden larger than 50 acres can often be attributed to him with little chance of contradiction.

Alan Mitchell (1922–   ).   The Patrick Moore of the tree world. A compulsive measurer of arboreal monsters, with a facility for quoting facts and figures on thousands of individual trees off the top of his head. Real one-upmanship if you can get him to measure a tree in your back garden.

Roy Lancaster (1937–   ).   Whizz-kid plant collector and compiler of *Hillier's Manual of Trees and Shrubs*. Spends most of the year following in the footsteps of Ernest 'Chinese' Wilson by leading treks to Nepal, Tibet and China. Lash out a few thousand pounds on one of these sorties to set yourself up at name-dropping for the rest of your life.

Beth Chatto (1923–   ).   Plantswoman *extraordinaire* whose garden and nursery near Colchester boast thousands of unusual plants. The most original female border designer since Gertrude Jekyll. Her books (see page 112) are treasured. Buy from her, read her, and talk to her at Chelsea Flower Show (she's a regular Gold Medal winner).

John Gerard (1518–1585).   Barber-surgeon whose *Herball* is revered by all avant-gardeners (even though it's full of fairy stories). He had a use for every plant (even the mandrake which, he said, screamed when uprooted). Fair knowledge; brilliant imagination.

Use your chosen names in phrases like: 'I can never agree with .... about dahlias.' 'Of course .... says it's not really tender at all.'

'Only the other day .... was showing me his border of them.'

And, best of all:

'Oh yes, that was given me by ....'

Place dropping

If you can't aspire to name dropping, place dropping is an adequate substitute. Simply visit the following gardens and drone on about them at length whenever the opportunity arises:

Sissinghurst Castle, Sissinghurst, Kent (the gardening Mecca).
Hidcote Manor, Hidcote Bartrim, Gloucestershire.
Powis Castle, Welshpool, Powys.
Great Dixter, Northiam, East Sussex.
Mottisfont Abbey, Mottisfont, Hampshire.
Nymans, Handcross, West Sussex.
Stourhead, Stourton, Wiltshire.
Bodnant, Tal-y-cafn, Gwynedd.
Crathes Castle, Banchory, Grampian.
Knightshayes Court, Tiverton, Devon.
Scotney Castle, Lamberhurst, Kent.
Wakehurst Place, Ardingly, West Sussex.
Savill Garden, Windsor Great Park, Berkshire.
Kiftsgate Court, Chipping Campden, Gloucestershire.

Crathes Castle in Grampian: a stately name to drop.

Where to Put Your Garden

It is not sufficient for a garden to be designed on avant-gardening lines. It must be situated in the right county if it is to have that all-important air of quality.

Fashionable counties
(*England & Wales*)
Gloucestershire
Kent
Sussex
Berkshire
Buckinghamshire
Cornwall
Devon
Hampshire
Suffolk
Oxfordshire
Powys
Somerset
Surrey
Wiltshire
Yorkshire

Fashionable counties
(*Scotland*)
Caithness
Sutherland
Wester Ross
Hebrides (Inner or Outer)

In London
Chelsea
Knightsbridge
Hampstead
Highgate
Barnes
Richmond
Kensington
Strand-on-the-Green
Kew

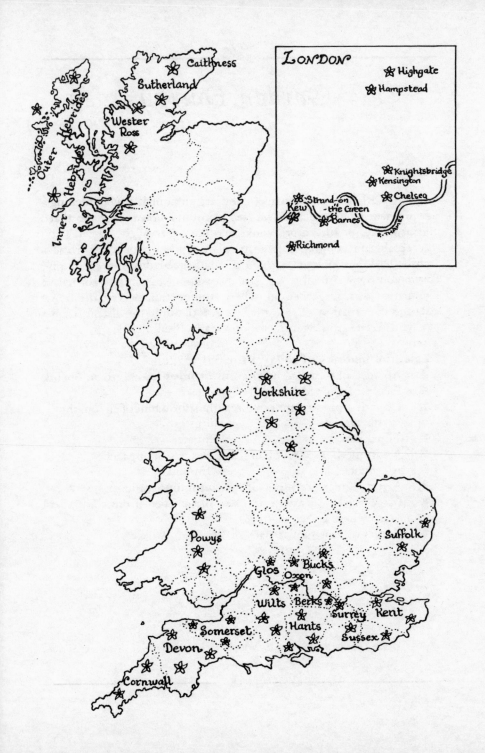

Garden Design

Avant-gardens are not made, they are designed, preferably by a prominent landscape architect (see below). Two or three years ago informality, or the natural look, was the order of the day. It's still acceptable in country cottage gardens, but formality has made a come-back and you are advised to adjust your design accordingly.

If you own a small town garden it should be entirely formal. If you own a large garden anywhere, the portion nearest the house should be formal. It's best if the rest is, too, but in the distant reaches of your estate, some return to informality is allowable.

Essential features of today's formal garden

- An allée of pleached hornbeams or limes leading to an obelisk
- Plenty of clipped box and yew
- Paths that run straight as a die with never a hint of an unfashionable curve
- Topiary
- A summerhouse (revolving) or, better still, a gazebo
- A croquet lawn
- A rectangular pool (not of the swimming variety)
- Large brick walls with doors in them (even if they don't lead anywhere or won't open)
- Gravel or rectangular slabs or bricks to walk on

No avant-garden is complete without its pleached allée. This one's at Hidcote.

The avant-gardener's nightmare: a rockery flanked by crazy paving.

Don't-touch-them-with-a-bargepole features

* Rockeries
* Putting greens
* Round, raised-up swimming pools
* Crazy paving
* Fibreglass goldfish pools
* Sheds (old stables and barns excepted)

- Aluminium greenhouses
- Plastic flowerpots, tubs and urns
- Interwoven fencing
- Corrugated lawn edging
- Integral barbecues
- Wrought ironwork (unless very old or ultra-modern)

Who designs it?

You can design the garden yourself (provided you say you were greatly influenced by some noted landscape architect or some noted garden). Better still, have a landscape architect in to do it for you. There's a great social cachet in upper class circles if your garden has been designed by:

- David Hicks – King of the straight line and the pleached allée.
- Peter Coats – Fond of Chinese Chippendale and white wood-work. Gardening Editor of *House & Garden*.
- Roddy Llewellyn – Trompe-l'oeil and town gardens a speciality.

The really serious minded (and the wealthy) go for:

- Russell Page – An acknowledged master. Designed Sir William Walton's garden on Ischia, and the garden at Royal Lodge, Windsor.
- Sir Geoffrey Jellicoe – Has designed landscapes as disparate as Chequers, Hemel Hempstead and Sutton Place.
- Dame Sylvia Crowe – Creator of several new towns, Banbury churchyard and the grounds of the Commonwealth Institute.

The serious-minded with more modest budgets can try:

- John Brookes
- Anthony du Gard Pasley
- David Stevens

All three design small gardens with great flair and their work can frequently be seen at Chelsea Flower Show.

Furniture and Ornaments

A well-designed garden can be ruined by badly chosen furniture and misplaced ornaments. Avoid the pitfalls, but don't think you'll escape criticism by doing without ornaments and putting the furniture away when you're not sitting on it. Avant-garde bits and pieces set the seal on an up-market garden.

Furniture for the avant-garden
Garden furniture need no longer be painted white. Several shades of soft blue-green (*eau de nil*, if you're in the know) are now highly fashionable and adorn features as avant-garde as the bridge in Monet's garden at Giverny.

Choose from:

Lutyens' design benches
Chinese Chippendale design benches
Old park benches
Old deck chairs
Plain wooden, steel or plastic furniture
Plain parasols

Furniture best smiled at and avoided
All-in-one table and bench units (highly efficient at grazing shins)
Aluminium 'wrought iron' table and chair sets
Rustic timber furniture (unless for a cottage garden)
Floral print anything
Swing seats
Garden furniture with excessive padding or on the scale of the stuff in 'Dallas'.
Old sewing machine tables with marble tops

Top marks for a Lutyens' design bench from the Charles Verey collection. Photo: Green Brothers (Geebro) Ltd.

Folding metal chairs from supermarkets
Teak furniture (unless it costs the earth and weighs a ton)

Ornaments for the avant-garden
Pergolas and gazebos
Sundials
Pillars from Coutts Bank (the old one in the Strand)
Lumps of stone and broken monuments
Rhubarb and seakale forcing pots in terracotta
Large terracotta pots
Chinese vases and Ali Baba jars

Collect terracotta rhubarb and seakale forcing pots purely as ornaments.

Old watering cans (no; not plastic ones)
Bridges over anything
Beehives (occupied or not)
Stone troughs and sinks and querns
Wire hanging baskets
Staddle stones (but *only* in country gardens)
Modern sculpture (especially by Henry Moore, Elizabeth Frink and
    Barbara Hepworth)
Large pebbles in groups
Topiary
Ancient statuary (but preferably not diaphanously draped damsels)
Decorative tops from redundant British Rail signals

Ornaments best sniffed at

Gnomes (be they plastic, stone, cement, concrete, standin', sittin',
   huntin', shootin', fishin' or anythin')
Plastic pots and urns
Concrete Venus de Milos
Street lamps
Bird baths
Bird tables
Frogs, toads, cats, herons and any other imitation animals
Plastic towerpots
Plastic hanging baskets
Wheelbarrows 'given a new lease of life' with summer bedding
Artificial wellheads
Half beer barrels 'given a new lease of life', etc.

Suppliers

Bill & Clare Marno, Towy Pottery, Rhandirmwyn, Llandovery,
   Dyfed.
   Terracotta flowerpots, rhubarb forcing pots and ceramic plant labels.
Green Brothers Ltd., Hailsham, East Sussex BN27 1BR.
   *Charles Verey garden furniture collection which includes Lutyens'
   designs.*
Ann's Garden, 37 Marsham Street, London SW1.
   Terracotta pots and urns.
Triconfort Ltd., Oak Street, Norwich, Norfolk.
   Classy garden furniture.
Haddonstone Ltd., The Forge House, East Haddon, Northants.
   Traditional stone ornaments.

Top-Notch Toolshed

The avant-gardener does not fill his or her garden shed with an armoury of stainless steel implements. Stainless steel is as out of place in the toolshed as it is on the tea tray. Look for robust and comfortable garden tools in tempered or forged steel and avoid gimmicky gadgets that will gather dust after their first foray into the wilderness.

Hereditary avant-gardeners need not buy a thing. It's far better to use the well-worn implements of your forefathers. Here's what you'll need:

SPADE
Top marks for models with an old, wooden 'D' handle. Second best is the wooden 'YD' shape. Maroon plastic handles don't cut much ice: 'T'-shaped handles cut blisters on your skin. Ladies are allowed to use a border spade which is slightly smaller than the regulation digging spade.

FORK
As for a spade (but avoid the flat-pronged potato fork which really belongs on the allotment). Border forks can be used even by beefy males if the soil is heavy.

RAKE
Good for smoothing over gravel drives.

DUTCH HOE
Superb to lean on. Not bad at weeding in between rows of vegetables and border plants. Very efficient at decapitating lilies and other fleshy-stemmed bulbs.

TROWEL
The only tool allowable in stainless steel. It should *not* bend.

Tell-tale signs of an avant-garden: builder's barrow, besom and Haws watering can.

WHEELBARROW

An unpretentious builder's barrow is by far the best buy (it's roomy and cheap). Galvanised Dinky Toy types are tolerable; plastic barrows with football-shaped wheels are definitely infra dig.

SECATEURS

Gardeners in the know buy Felco secateurs (even though they cost an arm and a leg). The makers guarantee them for life. A snip.

SHEARS

For cutting box and yew peacocks (use clattering electric versions for the privet).

WATERING CAN

Time was when the 'Haws' watering can graced every decent garden.

Nowadays the price will put you off. Still, you can always settle for the red plastic model instead of the russet-brown or galvanised job. Better still, go for a galvanised version of the old-fashioned watering can (the type Peter Rabbit jumped into). On no account settle for a £2 green plastic can. It doesn't look at all classy when carelessly left on the doorstep.

HOSEPIPE
Hide it.

Optional extras

WIRE-TOOTHED SPRINGBOK RAKE
For raking up leaves and hooking green slime out of the pool.

GARDEN LINE
For attempting to draw straight lines on the vegetable plot (it always seems to grow its own knots).

BESOM
(To be pronounced with care.) One of those witch's brooms that are difficult to use but which make you look as though you ought to know what you're doing.

SCYTHE
Watch your feet.

LOPPERS
Watch your fingers.

DIBBER
Watch your language (the butt of many a gardening joke). Supposedly made out of an old spade handle. Don't wait that long – buy a new one.

Not to be used
Certain implements are unmentionable as far as the avant-gardener is concerned:

HALF-MOON IRON
This has no connection with witchcraft, even though it looks like

the executioner's blade that used to swing over the man in the window at Madame Tussaud's. It's for chopping slivers of turf from the edge of your lawn to 'neaten it up' (not a phrase beloved of the avant-gardener). Used regularly over a period of years it can reduce a half-acre lawn to the size of a Turkish prayer mat.

EDGING SHEARS
Your plants should spill with gay abandon over your lawn edges. Edging shears are for public parks, along with half-moon irons, lobelia, alyssum, salvias and French marigolds (see **Beastly Blooms** on page 49).

Suppliers
Burton McCall Ltd., Samuel Street, Leicester.
    Felco secateurs.
Wilkinson Sword Ltd., Sword House, Totteridge Road, High Wycombe, Bucks.
Bulldog Tools, Clarington Forge, Wigan, Manchester.
Spear & Jackson, St. Paul's Road, Wednesbury, West Midlands.
Stanley Garden Tools Ltd., Woodhouse Mill, Sheffield, South Yorkshire.
Wolf Tools, Alton Road, Ross-on-Wye, Hereford & Worcester.

What to Wear

Avant-gardeners think carefully about what they wear for gardening. Practicality is important, but so is style. Nowhere in the garden is the Royal influence more noticeable than in clothing.

First of all, see below for the unacceptable garments you would not be seen dead in.

What not to wear – him
Galoshes, leather boots, shorts (even in blistering summers), mittens, blue nylon anoraks with mock-sheepskin collars, blue overalls, brightly patterned short-sleeved shirts (though when the weather's hot the sweater can come off and the long sleeves of your check shirt can be rolled up to just below the elbow (not above).

What not to wear – her
As for 'him', with the addition of: nylon ski pants, bikini in hot weather. Bermuda shorts are acceptable, provided they're not too bright.

Clothes for avant-gardeners
Now study the pages opposite and overleaf for your guide to *de rigueur* gardening wear.

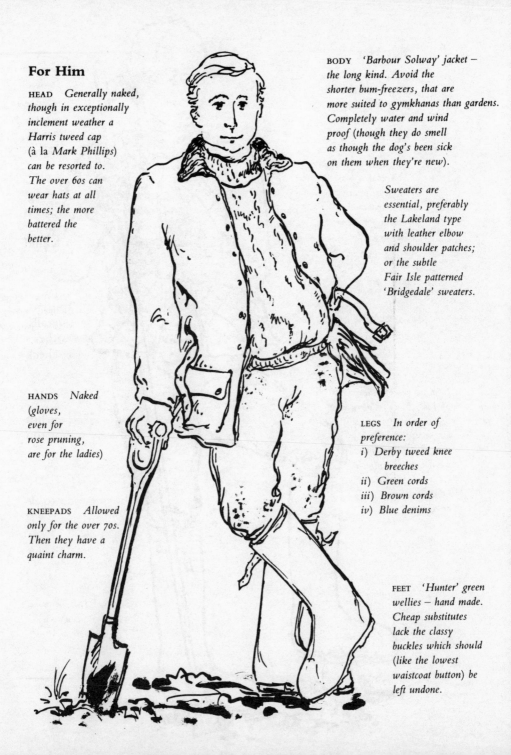

For Him

HEAD *Generally naked, though in exceptionally inclement weather a Harris tweed cap (à la Mark Phillips) can be resorted to. The over 60s can wear hats at all times; the more battered the better.*

BODY *'Barbour Solway' jacket — the long kind. Avoid the shorter bum-freezers, that are more suited to gymkhanas than gardens. Completely water and wind proof (though they do smell as though the dog's been sick on them when they're new).*

Sweaters are essential, preferably the Lakeland type with leather elbow and shoulder patches; or the subtle Fair Isle patterned 'Bridgedale' sweaters.

HANDS *Naked (gloves, even for rose pruning, are for the ladies)*

KNEEPADS *Allowed only for the over 70s. Then they have a quaint charm.*

LEGS *In order of preference:*
i) *Derby tweed knee breeches*
ii) *Green cords*
iii) *Brown cords*
iv) *Blue denims*

FEET *'Hunter' green wellies — hand made. Cheap substitutes lack the classy buckles which should (like the lowest waistcoat button) be left undone.*

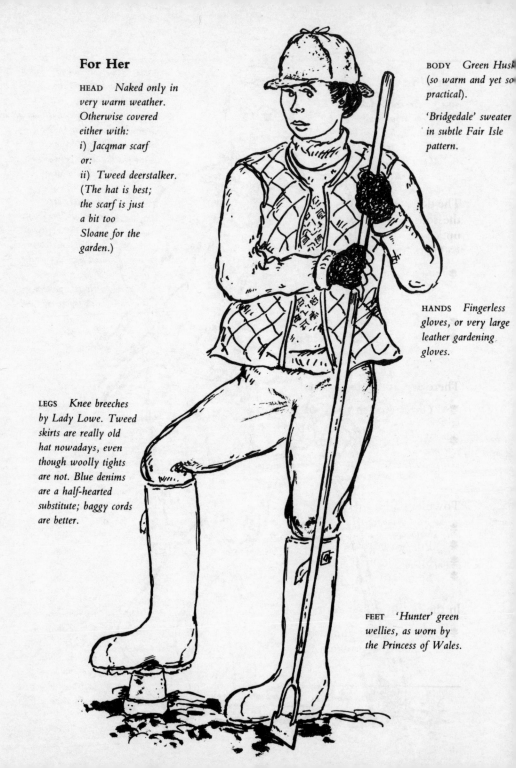

For Her

HEAD *Naked only in very warm weather. Otherwise covered either with:*
i) Jacqmar scarf
or:
ii) Tweed deerstalker. (The hat is best; the scarf is just a bit too Sloane for the garden.)

BODY *Green Husk (so warm and yet so practical).*

'Bridgedale' sweater in subtle Fair Isle pattern.

HANDS *Fingerless gloves, or very large leather gardening gloves.*

LEGS *Knee breeches by Lady Lowe. Tweed skirts are really old hat nowadays, even though woolly tights are not. Blue denims are a half-hearted substitute; baggy cords are better.*

FEET *'Hunter' green wellies, as worn by the Princess of Wales.*

Enriching Mother Earth

The dedicated avant-gardener is deeply conscious of his/her debt to the soil. Garden motto for all a-g's is: 'What goes in must come up.'

There are certain things you won't touch with a punt-pole:

* National Growmore (they dropped the 'National' bit years ago but old gardeners persist in reviving memories of 'Dig for Victory')
* Bonemeal (a waste of time and money)
* Sewage sludge (there's something unsavoury about growing tomatoes from pips people have passed)

There are other things you simply can't get enough of:

* Good garden compost (garden compost is always referred to as 'good')
* Well-rotted manure (always referred to as 'well-rotted' – preferably from your own horse so that you know just what it contains)

Townies will have to content themselves with acceptable substitutes:

* Peat (no nutrients but at least it's clean and readily available)
* Pulverised bark (best as a mulch to keep down weeds)
* Spent hops (it's good but it stinks)
* Spent mushroom compost (terrific stuff but a bit chalky)

In the fertiliser line your panacea for all ills is:

* Blood, bone and fishmeal (it really smells as if it's doing the plants a power of good, and, being organic, it keeps the

Blood, bone and fishmeal — the panacea for all plant ills.

bacteria going in the soil. The results really do seem to be better than those obtained with National Growmore)

* Sulphate of ammonia (high in nitrogen and quite useful for making your hedge grow quickly to screen you from the neighbours)
* Tomato fertiliser (bung it on anything that won't flower or fruit)

Digging it in

If you are madly keen and energetic you'll have a blitz on the soil once a year, during autumn and winter, forking in bulky manure on any bare spots (especially on the vegetable plot).

Laying it on

Sensible (and idle) avant-gardeners dig the soil and enrich it once; plant it up and then mulch for evermore. Mulching is one of the avant-gardener's favourite pastimes. It keeps down the weeds, it keeps in the moisture, it enriches the soil, and it's fashionable.

For appearances' sake, mulch with:

* Pulverised bark
* Peat
* Stable manure

To impress mulch with:

* Straw
* Newspaper
* Sawdust and shavings

The last three don't look very nice at all but they show you care about your plants.

The Annual Routine

Scatter good old blood, bone and fishmeal among shrubs and border plants in spring just before you mulch. That way your plants stay well-fed and watered for as long as possible.

When asked what you want for your birthday, reply: 'A trailer-load of manure.' Very avant-garde (especially when uttered by titled ladies).

Associations

If you want to be up to your arms in organic matter join:

The Henry Doubleday Research Association, Convent Lane, Bocking, Braintree, Essex.

The Soil Association, Walnut Tree Manor, Haughley, Stowmarket, Suffolk.

Both promote organic gardening with furious enthusiasm.

Garden Centre Guide

Those horticultural equivalents of Sainsbury's and Tesco's will lure you regularly into their clutches. Before you succumb to their blandishments remember your Garden Centre Alphabet. It should ensure the survival of both you and your plants.

A IS FOR ASSISTANTS   Rarer than loam. You'll come across three or four assistants when you don't want them. Like London buses, they always arrive in convoys but refuse to turn up when you need them.

B IS FOR BONEMEAL   Any salesman worth his salt will tell you it's essential at planting time. Ignore him. It will do little good except to make your wallet lighter.

C IS FOR CHECKOUT GIRLS   Now and again you'll find a little gem (horticulturally speaking). Again and again you'll find a demure poppet who knows as much about berberis as she does about brain surgery.

D IS FOR DORMANCY   You can expect deciduous trees to lack leaves between November and March. Become suspicious if they lack leaves in July.

E IS FOR EVERGREENS   Become suspicious if they lack leaves at any time.

F IS FOR FAMILY TREE   Aged nurserymen have a habit of telling you theirs when you enquire about an apple tree grafted with a number of varieties. The former can be fascinating; the latter disappointing.

G IS FOR GREENHOUSES   Usually groaning under the weight of hundreds of house plants. Rest assured that if you take home a tillandsia from a tropical temperature it will only languish in your lean-to loggia.

H IS FOR HEATHERS Sold in threes and tens in the belief that gardeners want to surround themselves with grouse moors.

I IS FOR INFORMATION See Assistants.

J IS FOR JAPANESE GARDEN A do-it-yourself kit comprising one bag of sand (to be raked), one bag of pebbles (to be arranged), two bamboos and a Japanese maple.

K IS FOR KNIFE All gardeners should have one. All garden centre assistants can close the gates faster than you can say it at five o'clock.

L IS FOR LABELS Guaranteed to tell you the name of the nurseryman, his address, postcode and telephone number. Occasionally the name of the plant may be visible, but usually it's faded.

M IS FOR MONEY You don't really need it. Any enterprising garden centre will take Access, American Express (says more about your plants than the checkout girl ever can) and Diner's Club.

N IS FOR NECROSIS Should the assistant diagnose an acute case of necrosis when you stagger back with a sickly plant, do not be impressed. He means it's dead.

O IS FOR ORGANIC GARDENING Known in the trade as muck and mystery. Becoming respectable because a few manufacturers are realising it's better to join 'em if you can't beat 'em.

P IS FOR PONDS Gigantic turquoise jelly moulds.

Q IS FOR QUICK 1) Hawthorn; 2) How garden centre owners get rich; 3) How to leave when your wife spots the house plant section.

R IS FOR ROOTBALL What all container-grown plants should possess. When lifted by its stem a container-grown plant should bring rootball and pot with it. Three spindly roots dangling in the breeze do not constitute a rootball.

S IS FOR SEX Should the assistant take offence when questioned about the sex of her hollies (only the females carry berries), find another nursery (or another assistant).

T IS FOR TOOLS A stupendous array. Impress your neighbours by taking home a brilliantly coloured implement that looks as though it was invented for bear-baiting. Never admit that you don't know what it's for.

D IS FOR DORMANCY *Beware the deciduous trees that lack leaves in July.*

U IS FOR USELESS   Try out the tool and you'll see what I mean.

V IS FOR VINES   Refuse to be convinced by an assistant who tells you: 1) They're dead easy to grow; 2) You can fit three into a 6 ft × 8 ft greenhouse; 3) You'll be drinking your own Beaujolais next year.

W IS FOR WEEDS   A few of them on the surface of the compost in a container-grown plant are a good sign of establishment. A forest of them are a highly efficient means of transferring our native flora to your garden.

X IS FOR EXTRA-SPECIAL OFFER   Plants that won't sell at any price. Often described as 'Plant of the Week'.

Y IS FOR YOUR LOCAL NURSERYMAN   Get to know him and he'll turn out to be a real gem who'll save you time, effort and money (even if he does go on a bit about the weather).

Z IS FOR ZZZZZZZZZ   An afternoon at the garden centre with armfuls of children and barrowfuls of plants and this is all you're fit for when you arrive back home.

Top Nurseries

The printed nursery labels that hang from the plants in your garden say as much about you as the labels in the back of your coat or jacket or dress (though it is as yet unknown for avant-gardeners to replace a plant label from Woolworths with one from a nursery equivalent of Harrods).

However, there is more than simple snobbery attached to buying plants. Any avant-gardener worth his or her salt will be proud of a choice and fashionable plant (see page 45) picked up on a market stall or even in a supermarket. But the 'in' nurseries are patronised because they, rather than anybody else, can be relied on to supply the 'in' plants. Here, then, are the nurserymen to patronise if you want to make sure of owning the plants that are high fashion:

❀ David Austin, Albrighton, Wolverhampton, W. Midlands.
　　Shrub roses and peonies
❀ Helen Ballard, Old Country, Mathon, Malvern, Worcestershire.
　　Hellebores and snowdrops
❀ Peter Beales, London Road, Attleborough, Norfolk.
　　Shrub roses
❀ Bressingham Gardens, Diss, Norfolk.
　　Especially border plants
❀ Broadleigh Gardens, Barr House, Bishop's Hull, Taunton, Somerset.
　　Dwarf bulbs
❀ Richard Cawthorne, 28 Trigon Road, London SW8.
　　Violas and violettas
❀ Beth Chatto, White Barn House, Elmstead Market, Colchester, Essex.
　　Unusual plants

- Edrom Nurseries, Coldingham, Eyemouth, Berwickshire.
  Alpines, hardy primulas, meconopsis
- Fisk's Clematis Nursery, Westleton, Saxmundham, Suffolk.
  Clematis
- Great Dixter Nurseries, Northiam, Rye, East Sussex.
  Clematis, shrubs, border plants
- R. Harkness & Co. Ltd., The Rose Gardens, Hitchin, Herts.
  Roses
- Hillier Nurseries, Ampfield House, Ampfield, Romsey, Hants.
  Trees and shrubs and other plants
- Hollington Nurseries Ltd., Woolton Hill, Newbury, Berks.
  Herbs
- W. E. Th. Ingwersen, Birch Farm Nursery, Gravetye, East Grinstead, West Sussex.
  Alpines
- Inshriach Alpine Plant Nursery, Aviemore, Scotland.
  Alpines
- John Mattock, Nuneham Courtenay, Oxford.
  Roses
- Ken Muir, Honeypot Farm, Weeley Heath, Clacton-on-Sea, Essex.
  Strawberries
- Nerine Nurseries, Welland, Worcestershire.
  Nerines
- Notcutts Nurseries, Woodbridge, Suffolk.
  Trees, shrubs and other plants
- Ramparts Nursery, Bakers Lane, Colchester, Essex.
  Silver and grey-leaved plants
- Scott's Nurseries, Merriott, Somerset.
  Fruit trees and bushes (many rare varieties)
- Suffolk Herbs, Sawyer's Farm, Little Cornard, Sudbury, Suffolk.
  Herb plants and seeds

Leave your classy labels dangling for all to see.

Christopher Lloyd,
GREAT DIXTER NURSERIES,
NORTHIAM,
SUSSEX.

❧ Van Tubergen, 304a Upper Richmond Road West, London
SW14.
Bulbs

All the above will supply by mail order.

Seedsmen
Apart from the handful of giants whose advertisements appear in everything from the *Radio Times* to the *Daily Star*, there are one or two other seedsmen who can supply oddities and rarities:

❧ Chiltern Seeds, Bortree Stile, Ulverston, Cumbria.
❧ D. T. Brown & Co. Ltd., Station Road, Poulton-le-Fylde, Blackpool.
❧ John Chambers, 15 Westleigh Road, Barton Seagrave, Kettering, Northants.
❧ J. W. Boyce, 67 Station Road, Soham, Ely, Cambridgeshire.

The Flower Garden

The people who remain convinced that fashion does not enter the garden can think again. Almost every year one or two plants go 'out' and others come 'in'. You'll have to be really on the ball to keep up, but here's what the gardener in the know raves about at the moment:

Favourite Flowers
You adore and plant masses of:

Old-fashioned shrub roses (even though they grow into monsters and have a three-week flowering season)
Grey and silver-leaved plants (the white garden at Sissinghurst is heaven to you)
Hellebores (you collect colour forms of *Helleborus orientalis* like a magnet collects nails)
Snowdrops (collect as many varieties as possible, even though you can't tell one from another)
Hostas (as for snowdrops)
Hemerocallis (to go with the hostas because there's now a society devoted to the two plants)

And plenty of:

Peonies
Pinks
Irises
Tobacco plants
Dahlias (Christopher Lloyd grows them in his mixed borders so that's the only place for them)
Clematis

Wisteria
Tropaeolums
Hardy annuals (so unpretentious and so pretty)
Melianthus major
Witch hazels
Rhododendrons (the Royal Horticultural Society's unofficial emblem)
Foxgloves
Ornamental grasses (except Pampas grass)
Ferns
Viburnums (but not the evergreen kinds)
Hollies
Lilies (essential)
Bamboos
Campanulas
Primulas
Euphorbias
Gunnera
Ornamental rhubarb
Eryngiums
Hardy geraniums
Eucalyptuses
Wallflowers
Fritillarias
Valerians
Sempervivums (in stone sinks and on roofs)
Hardy cyclamen
Hardy orchids
Fatsia japonica
Violets and pansies (but especially violets)
Rogersia
Cardoons
Hebes
Alchemilla mollis

Plant masses of hostas ...

Alliums
Colchicums
Crocuses (but not the large Dutch hybrids)
Nerines
Lavender
Cornflowers
Sweet peas (not those nasty knee-high jobs)
Penstemons
Love-in-a-mist
Lavateras
Camellias
Polygonums (except the Russian vine)
Any flowers that are green or brown

Beastly Blooms
To be avoided like the plague:

Gladioli
Chrysanthemums (except the annual kind)
Scarlet salvias (perennial salvias are all right)
French marigolds (pot marigolds are OK)
African marigolds
Afro-French marigolds (double the horror)
Hybrid tea roses (the occasional floribunda is acceptable)
Pampas grass (very suburban)
Leyland cypress (very, very suburban)
'Kanzan' cherry trees (those pink, street-side shuttlecocks. The white
    'Tai Haku' is the one for you – much more classy)
Petunias
Lobelia and alyssum in tandem (they're OK on their own)
Begonias (especially the dwarf bedding kinds)
Hyacinths
Nemesia
Mesembryanthemums
Annual asters

. . . and ferns.

Calceolarias
Ageratum
Heather and conifer beds (heathers belong on grouse moors)
Dwarf conifers
Double hollyhocks (single ones are fine)
Elaeagnus pungens 'Maculata'
Privet

Trees

'However small your garden, be sure to devote at least one acre to woodland,' said a Victorian garden designer. Follow the dictum if you can. If not, limit yourself to one tree that looks good in your garden and adds stature to an otherwise flat and shadeless vista.

Choose wisely, though. Plant no tree nearer to the house than 15 ft., and then make it a small one. Avant-gardeners have firm favourites, and even the trees they hate in town are generally acceptable when growing in massive gardens or country estates.

Here is the avant-gardener's list of favourites:

Whitebeam (*Sorbus aria* 'Lutescens')
Pocket handkerchief tree (*Davidia involucrata*)
Japanese maples (*Acer* species)
Mount Etna broom (*Genista aetnensis*)
Golden-leaved false acacia (*Robinia pseudoacacia* 'Frisia')
Snow gum (*Eucalyptus niphophila*)
Weeping silver-leafed pear (*Pyrus salicifolia* 'Pendula')
Irish yew (*Taxus baccata* 'Fastigiata')
Maidenhair tree (*Ginkgo biloba*)
Silver birch (*Betula* species, but *not* 'Young's Weeping')
Dawn redwood (*Metasequoia glyptostroboides*)
Brewer's weeping spruce (*Picea brewerana*)
White flowering cherry (*Prunus* 'Tai Haku')
Variegated poplar (*Populus* x *candicans* 'Aurora')
Golden Indian bean tree (*Catalpa bignonioides* 'Aurea')
Persian ironwood (*Parrotia persica*)
Black mulberry (*Morus nigra*)
Pillar apple (*Malus tschonoskii*)
Variegated tulip tree (*Liriodendron tulipifera* 'Aureomarginatum')
Golden rain tree (*Koelreuteria paniculata*)

Golden honey locust (*Gleditsia triacanthos* 'Sunburst')
Turkish hazel (*Corylus colurna*)
Variegated table dogwood (*Cornus controversa* 'Variegata')
Strawberry tree (*Arbutus unedo*)
Monkey puzzle (*Araucaria araucana* – preferably in a tub)
Lime and hornbeam (*Tilia* species and *Carpinus betulus* – for pleached allées)

Beastly trees for urban landscapes
Purple-leaved Norway maple (*Acer platanoides* 'Goldsworth Purple')
Copper beech (*Fagus sylvatica* 'Purpurea')
Pink flowering cherries (*Prunus* 'Kanzan' and 'Amanogawa')
Laburnum (*Laburnum watereri* 'Vossii') – unless trained over a pergola
Double pink hawthorn (*Crataegus oxyacantha* 'Paul's Double Scarlet')
Mount Atlas Cedar (*Cedrus atlantica glauca*)
Deodar (*Cedrus deodara*)
Golden weeping willow (*Salix* x *chrysocoma*)
Leyland cypress (x *Cupressocyparis leylandii*)
Young's weeping birch (*Betula pendula* 'Youngii')

Tree-upmanship with a variegated liriodendron.

Hedges

There's no interwoven fencing at Sissinghurst. Hedges are in and fences (except for the no-nonsense post-and-rail variety that surrounds farmland) are out. Take care, though. Not all hedges are desirable.

High-class hedges
Yew (*Taxus baccata*)   Slow and oppressively beautiful. The best peacock maker.

Box (*Buxus sempervirens*)   Superb for edging asparagus beds and herb gardens (for which you should use the dwarf variety 'Suffruticosa'). Better at making balls than peacocks.

Lavender (*Lavandula* species and varieties)   Very Gertrude Jekyll, so choose the variety 'Munstead' or, equally up-market, 'Hidcote'. Both are as good as their reputations.

Beech (*Fagus sylvatica*)   A stalwart of town gardens. A little overdone but still acceptable.

Ramanas rose (*Rosa rugosa*)   Dog- and neighbour-proof once it's thickened up. Crepe-paper-green leaves and pink, cerise or white flowers in summer. Excellent, but in danger of having its reputation sullied by tabloid newspaper advertisements which make extravagant claims on its behalf. Hybrid musk roses have not had such a bad press and are very up-market. Choose varieties like 'Cornelia' and 'Felicia'.

Western hemlock (*Tsuga heterophylla*)   A velvety-textured conifer as yet not much planted as a hedge. Quite avant-garde.

Dawn redwood (*Metasequoia glyptostroboides*)   Even more avant-

A holly hedge: boring as hell and hellish to weed under, but sets off your avant-garde sculpture.

garde, and expensive, too. A deciduous conifer thought to be extinct until it was rediscovered in China in the 1940s. Plant it for hedgeupmanship.

Hornbeam (*Carpinus betulus*)   Dreary but high class.

Laurel (*Prunus laurocerasus*)   The Victorians loved it. The Elizabethans hate it; all except those in the know. It's vigorous, fresh and shiny, and it will stand hard pruning. Good in town and country.

Spotted laurel (*Aucuba japonica*)   Loathed about ten years ago.

Coming back now. The critics have realised that any shrub with shiny, yellow-spotted, evergreen leaves that puts up with soot, smoke and insults can't be all bad.

Holly (*Ilex aquifolium*) Boring as hell and hellish to weed under, but smart and classless.

Tamarisk (*Tamarix gallica*) and Escallonia (*Escallonia* species) The hedges to choose if you live by the sea.

Last resort hedges

Privet (*Ligustrum ovalifolium*) The scourge of suburban gardens. Tatty, greedy and depressing. The ultimate 'last resort' hedge. The golden form is pretty but best when grown as a shrub, rather than a hedge.

Barberry (*Berberis* species) Eminently suited to cemeteries. Thorns that bed themselves irretrievably in your skin.

Hawthorn (*Crataegus monogyna*) In gardens bordering farms it's useful. Elsewhere in winter it looks like a jumble of rusty barbed wire.

Leyland cypress (x *Cupressocyparis leylandii*) Has made an excellent job of turning tiny suntrap gardens into dim grottoes in five years flat. For impatient troglodytes only.

Purple-leaved cherry (*Prunus* x *cistena*) A dwarf purple hedge that looks most at home with painted gnomes.

Copper beech (*Fagus sylvatica purpurea*) Oppressive. Shows off the white beech coccus (a sap-sucking pest) to great effect.

Evergreen small-leaved honeysuckle (*Lonicera nitida*) Poor man's box.

Golden bells (*Forsythia* species) Far too colourful to be classy.

Rhododendron (*Rhododendron ponticum*) Quite acceptable around Surrey golf courses and Surrey gardens, but elsewhere it is far too redolent of the stockbroker belt.

HEDGE CLIPPING

There's no cachet attached to hedge clipping and it's best if you can get 'a little man' to do it for you (see page 104). He will, hopefully, be armed with a spotless pair of shears and a square of sacking to gather up his clippings. However, he is more likely to be armed with electric trimmers and a large pair of feet. The former will leave clippings among your plants; the latter will leave footprints among your borders.

Climbers and Wall Plants

As a race, climbing plants are essential in the avant-garden. Naked brickwork, stonework or even pebbledash (though no avant-gardener would willingly live in a pebbledashed house) must be covered with leaves and, to some extent, flowers.

Avoid the common pitfalls. Do not entertain:

- White plastic trelliswork
- Green plastic trelliswork
- Wrought iron or plastic-coated arches
- Diamond-pattern trellis (it must be square)

Have lots of:

- Climbers growing through old fruit trees
- Climbers like clematis growing over steel hooped 'balloons'
- Climbers growing up rustic pole tripods
- Climbers growing up columns made from greeny-blue painted trellis
- Climbers on colonnades (poles linked by swags of rope)
- Climbers on gazebos

When you've equipped yourself with the acceptable support systems you'll have to choose the right plants.

Avant-garde climbers and wall plants

Abutilon vitifolium (preferably mixed with *Solanum crispum* 'Glasnevin', as at Wisley)
Vines (especially *Vitis coignetiae*)
Actinidia kolomikta (for its pink leaf tips)
Magnolia grandiflora

You adore clematis – but only on squared trellis (no diamonds).

Tropaeolum (any)
Ribes speciosum
Ceanothus
Clematis (especially *C. macropetala, C. viticella, C. orientalis, C. tangutica* and – best of all – *C. cirrhosa balearica*)
Roses (only single-flowered varieties, especially 'Mermaid')
Cytisus battandieri
Wisteria (but only if it's old)
Sweet peas
Fremontodendron californicum
Ivy (except the varieties 'Gold Heart' and 'Buttercup')
Humulus lupulus 'Aureus' (Golden hop – especially good at Hidcote growing up a copper beech hedge)
Solanum crispum 'Glasnevin' (see abutilon)

Climbers to be avoided in avant-gardens
Wisteria (if it's young)
Clematis 'Jackmanii' (pronounce it 'Jackmarny' and you're really out in the cold)
Pyracantha (firethorn)
Chaenomeles (Japanese quince)
Garrya (dreary grey tassels and drearier green leaves)
Polygonum baldschuanicum (Russian vine or mile-a-minute. A thug)
Passiflora (Passion flower, now rather too common for its own good)
Forsythia
Ivy in the varieties 'Gold Heart' and 'Buttercup' (they're now trained over interwoven fencing too frequently)
Roses (double-flowered varieties, especially 'Handel')

Roses

The old-fashioned shrub rose is the national emblem of the avant-gardener. No matter that most shrub roses grow into monsters; that most of them have just a three-week flowering season in late June and early July, and that most of them are cruelly barbed and play hell with your Lakeland knitwear. They are essential.

When quizzed on the advisability of devoting most of your garden to them, reply to the effect that they have:

- Old world charm
- Fascinating histories
- Unparalleled scents
- Beautifully shaped flowers
- Attractive heps (*not* hips)
- Disease-free foliage (but pray they don't see the mildew on your *Rosa Mundi*)

There really are no bad shrub roses as far as the dedicated avant-gardener is concerned, though if you're wise you'll leaven your collection with repeat-flowering modern shrub roses that have the charm of their forebears and a facility for keeping you amused longer. This is quite acceptable socially.

Learn to chat about a few of the groups into which old roses fall:

- Gallicas
- Hybrid musks
- Hybrid perpetuals
- Albas
- Centifolias
- Moss roses
- Damasks
- Bourbons

Every avant-garden has its shrub roses – watch the sun shine through the scarlet thorns of Rosa omeiensis pteracantha.

Grow one or two rose hedges, and take rose cuttings each autumn so that you can pass on old rarities to your friends. Do not grow your roses in 'rose beds'. They belong in the mixed border (see page 65).

There are hundreds of obscure varieties available from Peter Beales and David Austin (see page 41 for addresses) and you should aim to grow at least three or four that none of your friends possess.

The euphony of old rose names is (secretly) half the reason for their being so popular. If you want to impress, I recommend the following varieties as being particularly avant-garde when tripped lightly off the tongue:

- Assemblage des Beautés
- Félicité Parmentier
- Blanc Double de Coubert

The avant-gardener's bedside books.

- Belle de Crécy
- Cardinal de Richelieu
- Gruss an Aachen
- Tour de Malakoff
- Souvenir de Philémon Cochet
- Mme de Sancy de Parabère
- Baron Girod de l'Ain

You have two 'bibles' on your bookshelf: *The Old Shrub Roses*, and *Shrub Roses of Today*, both by Graham Stuart Thomas, who is to blame for bringing back these delightful old charmers.

HYBRID TEA ROSES

Do not be tempted into planting any of them (their new name of 'large-flowered roses' gives the game away; they're blowsy and vulgar). Flower show fodder.

FLORIBUNDA ROSES

Slightly more acceptable than hybrid teas, but don't plant too many or their masses of bloom will detract from your shrub roses.

MINIATURE ROSES

Neither fish nor foul. Bred for windowboxes and borders alongside patios, which is all they are fit for. (No avant-gardener worth his/her salt could have truck with any plant that can be pruned with a pair of scissors.)

Beds and Borders

Preferably borders. Beds are acceptable provided they are large enough, but do not be tempted to spatter your lawn with 4-ft. diameter circles. When Alan Bloom (see page 111) talks about island beds he does not mean beds like traffic islands; he's thinking more on the lines of Corsica or Sicily. Make your beds large and your borders wide.

Time was when the herbaceous border reigned supreme; then it took a nosedive in popularity because some spoilsport suggested it was labour-intensive. Gardeners are now realising that all gardening is labour-intensive so they might just as well have a herbaceous border and enjoy the summer colour.

But it is the 'mixed border' that is most predominant in avant-gardens. It contains shrubs, the odd tree, odder foliage plants, border perennials and bulbs and annuals in season. It's a sensible idea. The plants show themselves off well and there's nearly always something to look at whatever time of year. The whole mixture is leavened with a hefty helping of shrub roses (best grown in and among the other plants so that when they are out of flower (for eleven months of the year) you need not stare at barren branches).

Avant-gardens do not contain flower beds especially created for spring and summer bedding. These belong on the aforementioned traffic islands. Bedding plants are fitted in to pockets of soil (fairly roomy pockets) known as 'drifts', which are left between the shrubs and border perennials.

It's fashionable to plan different colour schemes for these drifts every year and to experiment with horrendously vibrant shades of orange and magenta. At least half your summer bedding plants should be ornamental vegetables. Try:

- Ornamental cabbage (the only one the avant-gardener grows)

At least half your summer bedding plants should be ornamental vegetables.

- Swiss and ruby chard
- Beetroot (only for its pretty leaves)
- Purple-podded pea
- Leeks (beautiful foliage plants)

Very few shrubs in the mixed border should be allowed to grow on their own. Train climbers through them to add colour when the shrubs' blooms are past it or not yet up to it. Use the Viticella or Macropetala clematises for preference.

Cram your beds and borders to bursting point. Soil is a dirty word in the flower garden and you shouldn't be able to see a bit of it.

THE COWARD'S WAY OUT
Should the placing of plants be a nightmare to you, there is an easy alternative. Designate all your beds and borders as one-colour schemes. A white-border, a green border, a red border, etc., will enable you to plant away feverishly once you've chosen your colour. There's only one drawback: the view can be hellish boring.

Rock Gardening

If you're a lover of alpines (those little plants from lofty places), hard luck. They're not really accepted by trend-setting avant-gardeners, probably because it's impossible to eradicate from the mind the vision of that mound of grey dust that's studded with lumps of broken concrete and called a 'rockery' by lovers of aubrieta and arabis.

Try to think of one stately home that has a rockery in its garden and you'll be hard pushed to come up with anything.

The place to see a real rock garden is Wisley, the home of the Royal Horticultural Society. All avant-gardeners are members and so get in free (along with a friend or two). Here several thousand tons of sandstone have been laid very correctly (tilting slightly backwards with their horizontal strata all running in the same direction) on an acre or more of sloping ground. There's little room for plants among the stones but alpine growers seem to like it that way.

Really enthusiastic avant-gardeners can build a miniature copy of Wisley's job in their back garden, but only if they have the in-depth knowledge to back up their dabbling. (Unfashionability can be countered to some extent by an admission of an insatiable appetite for a specialist group of plants.)

There are ways round the problem. Instead of imitating nature (and, after all, nobody is going to believe that the rocky outcrop in your garden is a natural phenomenon when you live in darkest Mortlake), create an obviously artificial feature for your alpines. Raised brick or stone beds two or three feet high can be built 'dry', filled with well-drained earth and grit and then planted up. A top-dressing of grit is essential too and separates the enthusiasts from the dabblers.

Lumps of tufa are very 'in'. These hunks of stone are the result

The acceptable face of rock gardening.

of calcium carbonate deposits and make avant-garde free-standing features when crevices are chipped out of them and planted up with cushion-forming alpines.

Even better are old stone sinks, horse troughs and querns. These are *very* avant-garde and any garden (even Sissinghurst) can boast them with pride. Plant them up with house leeks (*Sempervivums*), saxifrages and the like.

The ultimate enthusiast will have an 'alpine house' (made especially by C. H. Whitehouse Ltd., Buckhurst Works, Frant, Tunbridge Wells, Kent) in which they can shelter their treasures (the ones that hate damp, British winters).

One-upmanship among alpine gardeners is rife, and there is a certain cachet involved in growing certain plants. There's one snag here; only skill will ensure you come out tops. Alpine gardening is no sport for the dilettante who simply wants to boast.

Accomplished gardeners who want to test their skill and grow plants to impress should try:

Aretian androsaces
Paraquilegia grandiflora
Dionysias
Petiolarid primulas (especially in the Home Counties)
Primula allionii
Gentiana acaulis (and flower it every year)
Cypripediums (and flower them every year)
Ramondas, Haberleas and Jankaeas

If you can't be bothered with all this lot there is a simple alternative. Obtain one plant of *Eritrichium nanum*, grow it in a pot and flower it every year for five years. You'll then be accepted as the best alpine gardener ever.

If all these names are Greek to you, alpine gardening is not your forte. Go on to the next chapter.

Water Gardening

Lakes are best. Large pools of informal design are tolerable. Turquoise jelly-mould pools are unmentionable. Formal canals are unsurpassable.

Do remember that water gardens are designed to show off water – not a lawn of duckweed or fairy floating moss. A few water lilies add a touch of class but too many of them will rob your lake of its reflective qualities.

Do not line your pool with concrete; it fractures and leaks at least three times a year. Do not line your pool with turquoise PVC; it is not a public swimming bath. Line your pool with black butyl rubber – it makes the pool look deep and reflective and it lasts for donkeys' years.

With formal gardening on the up and up, long, rectangular pools are the most avant-garde. Edge them with thick York stone flags (not bits of crazy paving). A few goldfish are allowed but stick to golden orfe, not those hideously marked Japanese Koi carp for which you'll have to take out a second mortgage and insure at a high premium against herons with no taste.

Consider with care the purchase of a fountain. If it's like the one in Geneva all well and good. If it looks like a small leak from a water pipe forget it. *No* spurting statuary (unless it's genuine bronze), especially that young, bad-mannered youth from Belgium.

The only kind of lighting that's acceptable is floodlighting from above the pool. Do not submerge those red, green, blue and yellow disco lights in the water. They'll make your pool look like the Regent's Park aquarium.

If there's little room in your garden for a series of full-blown waterworks to rival those at Chatsworth, keep it simple. Fit a wall-mounted fountain where a lion's head can regurgitate water into a

Millstone, water and obligatory a–g labrador.

terracotta bowl. The arrangement might look as though it once contained holy water in a place of worship, but it's never-the-less fashionable.

Where children play and safety is important, construct a water feature from an old millstone or grindstone so that the water is sent up through the hole in the middle to spill over the stone and back into a sunken reservoir from whence it is recirculated. There's no depth of water in which children could drown (though they can quite easily fracture their skulls if they fall on to the stone).

Suppliers

Anglo Aquarium Plant Co. Ltd., Wayside, Cattlegate Road, Enfield, Middlesex.
    Butyl liners

Highlands Water Gardens Nurseries, Solesbridge Lane, Chorley-wood, Herts.
    Equipment and plants

Lotus Water Garden Products Ltd., 260/300 Berkhamsted Road, Chesham, Bucks.
    Equipment and plants

Wildwoods Water Gardens Ltd., Theobalds Park Road, Crews Hill, Enfield, Middlesex.
    Equipment and plants

Stapeley Water Gardens Ltd., Stapeley, Nantwich, Cheshire CW5 7LH.
    Equipment, plants and fish

Vegetable Growing

You *must* grow your own vegetables and bore your friends to death with the current state of your broccoli/Swiss chard/mangetout peas/zucchini. Smile knowingly when they question the economic viability of such a pastime (the flavour makes up for the fact that, labour included, your mangetouts have cost you 40p a pod).

There really is no flavour like home-grown vegetables, pock-marked by flea beetles, scallopped by pea and bean weevils and riddled with wireworm holes.

Grow your vegetables on an allotment if you are really dedicated and lacking in space at home. ('The local allotment chaps are so helpful, and they do seem fascinated by my asparagus peas, salsify and scorzonera.')

Only on the allotment should you grow your vegetables in rows. In the garden things should be organised differently. Grow your vegetables in the flower border (see page 65) if space is really short. Otherwise turn your vegetable patch into a potager, and let drop a few telling comments:

'I do so love Rosemary Verey's potager at Barnsley House; don't you?'
'It was Joy Larkcom who told me that polyanthus flowers are edible.'

The potager idea (a sort of French knot garden with a patchwork quilt of vegetables) is actually quite useful. Ostensibly it enables you to have a good-looking vegetable plot with colourful varieties of lettuce and the like showing one another off. What it also does (thanks to the brick, gravel or sawdust paths) is make a pretty pattern even if your vegetables are a dead loss.

Organic gardening (if you can understand it) is highly recommended on the vegetable plot. Crop spraying is not something for

No rows in the avant-vegetable-garden — everyone's gone potager.

the avant-vegetable-gardener. The vegetables should be fresh and dew-laden when picked and it really doesn't matter if they are greenfly-laden too (provided your water tap emits a fairly strong jet to squirt them off).

Grow plenty of tagetes (the only time you should ever grow French marigolds) to plant between your capsicums and suchlike to repel whitefly. (It's a vain hope but it shows willing.) Make sure, too, that there's lots of catch-cropping and intercropping going on. Plan your vegetable colour schemes with all the flair of a Jekyll or a Chatto.

But most important of all, grow the right crops:

Avant-garde vegetables
Salads (also known as Saladini, but no relation of that anti-Crusader Egyptian sultan)

Lettuces (in all their coloured and cut-leafed varieties)
Broccoli (the only brassica you should grow)
American or land cress
Swiss chard
Runner beans
Mangetout peas
Asparagus peas (inedible but classy)
Purple-podded peas
Chicory (lots of coloured-leafed types)
Zucchini (green and yellow)
Salsify and scorzonera (even if you're not sure how to cook or eat them)
Kohlrabi (sounds like an Eastern potentate; tastes like a cross between cabbage and turnip)
Globe artichokes
Jerusalem artichokes
Chinese artichokes
Asparagus (be patient)
Aubergines and capsicums ('we do so adore moussaka and ratatouille')
French beans
Celeriac
Chinese cabbage (the only cabbage – apart from ornamental varieties – you should grow)
Endive
Curly kale (for steaming, not boiling)
Early potatoes (just a few; preferably a rare variety from Donald MacLean, Dornock Farm, Crieff, Perthshire)
Leeks
Onions
Garlic
Parsnips
Radishes
Rhubarb (under terracotta forcing pots)
Seakale (as for rhubarb)
Spinach (even though you hate the taste)

Florence fennel (even though it's hard as nails)
Tomatoes

And do grow a few edible flowers to shock the uninitiated:

Pot marigolds
Nasturtiums
Polyanthus
Violets
Borage (you'll never get rid of it once it's sown)
Dwarf double daisies

Vegetables to spurn
Cabbages
Brussels sprouts
Cauliflowers
Carrots
Beetroots
Ridge cucumbers
Turnips and swedes
Maincrop potatoes
Pumpkins
Sweet corn
Celery
Broad beans

Your bibles are *The Vegetable Garden Displayed* (published by the Royal Horticultural Society), and *The Salad Garden* by Joy Larkcom.

Order common seeds from the larger merchants, and the rarities from Suffolk Herbs, Chiltern Seeds, or John Chambers (addresses on pages 42 and 44).

Herb Gardening

You can't fail with herbs. Every single one of them is fashionable. What you must do, though, is grow them in a formal plot all by themselves. Brick or gravel or York stone paths should criss-cross the plot so that it looks like an Elizabethan knot garden or a seventeenth-century parterre (it doesn't matter that you don't understand these terms, provided you bandy them about confidently).

Plant your herbs in drifts and patches and make sure you include medicinal varieties to add colour as well as scent and flavour provided by the culinary types.

Sissinghurst boasts a large vat of sempervivums in its herb garden. Copy it or invent something similar.

Chamomile seats are very in – fill a brick 'box' with earth, plant it up with 'Treneague' chamomile and make arms and a backrest out of dwarf box. Chamomile lawns are good, too, but a pain in the back when it comes to weeding.

Herbs you must grow
Tarragon (French, *not* Russian which is supposed to have an inferior
  flavour. *Entente* wins over *detente*.)
Basil
Dill
Rosemary
Sorrel
Fennel (purple or green)
Thyme (in 38 varieties from Hollington Nurseries)
Mint (in a sunken bucket in 12 varieties)
Parsley (as an edger – if you can get it to come up)
Chives (giant and small)
Rocket
Angelica (if you've room)

Herbs are a must in pot or garden.

If you've no room, grow your herbs in terracotta pots on steps, windowsills or a terrace (avant-gardeners do not have patios).

Fruit Growing

For some inexplicable reason there is no cachet attached to fruit growing in the avant-garden. This means that the bushes or whatever must be grown in one of two ways:

- In a netted fruit cage on the lines of the Snowdon aviary at Regent's Park, which is hidden away behind banks of holly and laurel.
- Among shrubs and flowers in the ornamental part of the garden.

There are one or two exceptions:

- Peaches are a must in the conservatory, or on a 'warm wall'.
- Figs are a must on a warm wall or in the conservatory.
- Strawberries may be grown in terracotta pots on the terrace (tower pots are for patios)
- Ancient apple varieties (from Scott's of Merriott – see page 42 for address) may be planted to make an orchard.
- Gooseberry bushes (even standard ones) can be used as features in vegetable and herb gardens.
- A mulberry is essential – preferably surrounded by a tree seat and preferably very old.
- A nuttery (planted with cobnuts and filberts) is impeccably avant-garde.
- Vines are most highly esteemed when of considerable age and when they are growing in a huge conservatory, tended by a gnarled gardener. Outdoors they are regarded as ornamental plants.

Drearies
Blackcurrants (reds and whites are acceptable in vegetable and herb gardens)

A mulberry is essential – preferably surrounded by a tree seat and preferably very old.

Loganberries, wineberries and all beastly hybrid berries
Thornless blackberries (you gather yours wild in the hedgerows and
   to hell with the scratches)
Raspberries are tolerated because they're good to eat, but hide them.

Ancient fruit trees

These are *never* chopped down. Instead they are decorated with swags of rambling roses which are trained up through them. 'Kiftsgate' is a favourite (and an embarrassing mistake if your garden is on the small side). Clematis is useful, too, as are vines.

Rose-covered trees are superb garden features until they fall down. Then you'll find yourself with the doubly difficult job of hacking to bits a gnarled old tree riddled with thorny stems that swipe at you like some barbed triffid.

The Lawn

Avant-gardeners do not have lawns; they have grass. But not much. The 'bowling green' lawn is a feature that belongs in front of council houses where it is surrounded by borders of lobelia, alyssum, French marigolds and salvias with standard fuchsias used as 'dot plants'.

The avant-gardener's grass is intermingled with daisies, plantains, buttercups, speedwell, pearlwort, dandelions and plenty of moss (usually at least 50% of the total coverage). This is a state of affairs to be encouraged.

The grass is mown (avoiding a striped effect at all costs) once a week at the height of summer with a rotary mower or a Flymo (if you can get it to start).

The existing flora of the 'lawn' should be improved with a mixture of wild flower seeds to prove that you are doing your bit to bring back the native flora: Obtain seeds from:

❧ John Chambers, 15 Westleigh Road, Barton Seagrave, Kettering, Northants
❧ Suffolk Herbs, Sawyer's Farm, Little Cornard, Sudbury, Suffolk

Gardeners with large plots should devote a good sized area to unmown grass where wild flowers and bulbs can be allowed to flourish. The more this site is criticised by tidy gardeners the better. A bit of name-dropping will get you out of tight corners. Try:
'Christopher Lloyd does it at Dixter, you know.'

For details of when to cut your carpeting botanic garden see *The Well-Tempered Garden*, by Christopher Lloyd.

Avant-gardeners do not make 'lawns' from turf. It is permissible

Plenty of daisies and not a stripe in sight on the avant-gardener's lawn.

to sow grass seed, but rather better to mow whatever comes up naturally so that the mixed flora is encouraged.

Grass mazes
Don't forget that grass mazes are now even more fashionable than those made from hedges. Copy patterns from ancient tomes, or invent them yourself. In this instance turf can be used for the paths, interspersed with brick or gravel to make the chosen pattern.

Warning
NEVER use lawn weedkillers, and if you must use a fertiliser to green up your sward, choose an organic one such as blood, bone and fishmeal to help hang on to your wild flowers. Better still, use nothing at all.

Your rotary lawn mower (preferably *not* one of those plastic vacuum cleaner jobs) should be the only implement you need. Spurn both edging shears and half moon irons (see page 28). Lawn rakers, fertiliser distributors and spiked aerators are for the 'bowling green' crowd.

Lawn pests and diseases are totally ignored, and 'fairy rings' positively encouraged (children love them).

Town Gardening

You don't need rolling acres to become an avant-gardener. Designed and planted up in line with avant-gardening principles, even a windowbox can speak volumes about its owner.

The basic rules of avant-gardening still apply (see the pages on design and choosing plants), but there are certain embellishments that will lift a town garden out of the ordinary:

- Trompe l'oeil – artificial window frames nailed to walls and backed with mirrors to create an illusion of space (beloved of vain gardeners and Roddy Llewellyn)
- Emphasis of shape – it's old hat to disguise the shape of your garden. If it's long and thin make it look longer and thinner by planting an avenue of lime trees down each side. (It doesn't matter that in five years' time you'll have no light and that everything under the trees will be sticky thanks to the honeydew-secreting aphides above; it's fashionable.)
- Evergreens (to give the garden year-round framework). Camellias and hebes are favourites.
- No lawn (unless it's chamomile).
- Plenty of rectangular York stone paving ('from that nice man on the council who only charged me £50'), gravel and pebbles.
- A plethora of pots (terracotta) and sinks (stone or 'hypertufa' – a mixture of sand, peat, cement and water that is used to cover white porcelain sinks to make them look like stone).
- A tree (just the one). See page 51 for choice.
- Herbs – everywhere.
- An arbour (the poor man's gazebo).

- ❧ Plants from Chelsea Flower Show (stagger back home with them on the Friday night, hoping that the tube train doors won't decapitate the delphiniums).
- ❧ Windowboxes and hanging baskets (*not* plastic)
- ❧ Plants with 'architectural form' (anything totally lacking in grace – *Mahonia* 'Charity' and the like).
- ❧ Hostas and ferns.

Totally out in town

Hammocks
Rotary clothes lines (go to the launderette)
Plastic pots and windowboxes
Ostentatious barbecues
Rustic furniture
Screen-block walling (you are not in Spain now)
Ranch-style fencing (you are not in Dallas now)
Interwoven fencing (you are not in prison now)
Well heads (Italian or English)
Female statues (any nationality)
Mock balustrades
Pulverised bark paths
Rock gardens
Plastic trug baskets
Neo-Georgian coach lamps
Concrete
Crazy paving
Topiary (except balls and cones)

Adjust your dress

The recommended garden wear suggested on pages 31 and 32 is rather over-the-top for town gardening. Do not feel tempted to tend your Wandsworth windowbox dressed in Barbour jacket and green Hunter wellies. Everyday leisure wear is acceptable in favourable weather, with the addition of a sensible waterproof in case of showers.

A Japanese maple in a Chinese pot – an elegant town garden ornament.

Town gardeners do not go out in really foul weather, so seldom need the full protection of their country counterparts who insist on braving it.

Avant-gardeners with both town and country properties should make sure that they are in the right frame of mind for the garden they happen to be tending at the moment, and that the correct wardrobe is to hand.

The Conservatory

A greenhouse is not something to boast about. It's a utilitarian garden feature best hidden behind a bank of shrub roses.

The conservatory, on the other hand, is something to flaunt. The bigger your conservatory, the better.

You treat your conservatory rather like a winter garden. It's a room of the house where plants happen to grow out of the floor, and it has an air of grandeur and plenty about it. Meals are taken in the conservatory whenever possible – breakfast especially – and a suite of wicker furniture fitted with comfortable cushions is *de rigueur*.

But there are pitfalls. Make sure your conservatory is a custom-built model with white woodwork and, if possible, decorative finials. Curved-eaved lean-to greenhouses are not conservatories.

The floor is best quarry tiled, with narrow soil borders left to grow climbing plants. Rush mats are tolerable but that's all.

On no account include
Parrots on perches
Budgerigars in cages
Tropical fish in tanks
Macramé pot hangers
Algae-encrusted fountains and waterfalls
Coloured lights (plain spotlights are acceptable)

Plants to avoid
Tuberous begonias (unless you enjoy honest vulgarity)
Orchids (unless you enjoy dishonest vulgarity)

Sinningias (Gloxinias)
Tomatoes, cucumbers and capsicums (they belong in the greenhouse)

Plants to plant
Tropical and sub-tropical climbers (especially the up-market Jade
    vine)
Bananas
Coffee and tea (but don't expect to be self-sufficient)
Geraniums (Pelargoniums) and all house plants on page 93
Clivias
Strelitzia (bird of paradise flower)
Palms
Cycads
Pawpaws
Bamboos
Peaches
Figs
Melons

Management
You may have to do it yourself, but it's far better if you can inveigle
an elderly (and preferably grumpy) gardener to tend your tropical
treasures for you. They'll need regular hosing, feeding and cherishing
if you want to emulate the atmosphere of the Palm House at Kew.

Suppliers
Amdega Ltd., Faverdale Industrial Estate, Darlington, Co. Durham.
Machin Designs, 4 Avenue Studios, Sydney Close, London SW3.
Room Outside Ltd., Goodwood Gardens, Waterbeach, Chichester,
    West Sussex.

Take breakfast in your conservatory (see previous page). Photo: Amdega Limited.

House Plants

It's not easy to find avant-garde house plants. Most of them are extremely un-avant. When used at all they should provide a pleasant, light-weight verdure; not a dense thicket through which lost Japanese soldiers might be expected to emerge at any moment.

Avant-garde house plants
Lilies (while in bloom)
Schizanthus
Geraniums (Pelargoniums)
Large palms
Asparagus ferns
Other ferns
Stephanotis
Hoya
Cordyline (but not Dracaena)
Vallota
Aspidistra
Arum lilies
Ficus benjamina
Cineraria
Gardenia
Calceolaria
Brunfelsia
Clivia
Jasminum
Citrus
Grevillea
Primulas

Your asparagus fern will strike the right note standing in a large antique bowl.

Un-avant-garde house plants
Hippeastrum (amaryllis)
Stag's horn fern
Dieffenbachia
Philodendron
Cacti & succulents
Christmas cacti
Croton (Joseph's coat)
Monstera
Bromeliads (all relations of the pineapple)

Chrysanthemums
Aphelandra
Sinningia (Gloxinia)
African violets (Saintpaulias)
Impatiens (busy lizzie)
Ficuses (rubber plants)
Venus fly traps
Azaleas
Large-flowered begonias
Bonsai anything

Seldom acknowledge your house plants. Water them rarely and feed them only occasionally in summer. Most of them will enjoy an annual repotting in spring. Don't wax lyrical about them in front of visitors as you would the shrub roses in the garden. House plants are looked upon as furniture and, as such, it's bad form to discuss their quality.

Pot hiders
Plants look good in fireplaces (preferably when there's no fire, unless you've taken to growing tuberous begonias and sinningias which, say some, should be burned anyway), on tables and on pedestals. Large bowls (preferably antique) will help to mask pots and prevent ring-marks on polished mahogany. Large wicker baskets can contain plants that stand on the floor.

Do not under any circumstances suspend your plants in macramé hangers. These confections of knotted rope belong in Chinese restaurants.

Flower Arranging

In general this is not be encouraged. Flowers in the house are a must, but the avant-gardener is a fan of bunches and posies, not of writhing works of art that are 50 per cent oasis, 25 per cent driftwood, 20 per cent leaves and 5 per cent flowers.

Flowers are best plonked (never admit that they are 'arranged' – something that happens to cats) in large bowls or vases. They should not be placed on pedestals, except in large or stately homes, and then, never on wrought iron ones, except in church.

Refuse to entertain anything to do with Ikebana (what passes for Japanese floral art), and if you can only find two flowers in the entire garden, stick them in a drinking glass on their own – not in a pin-holder stood in a saucer along with three iris leaves and five smooth pebbles.

Very avant-garde flowers for bunching	Un-avant-garde flowers for arranging
Lilies	Gladioli
Peonies	Dahlias
Lilies	Gladioli
Anemones	Chrysanthemums
Lilies	Gladioli
Poppies	
Lilies	
Hardy annuals	
Lilies	
Spring bulbs	
Lilies	

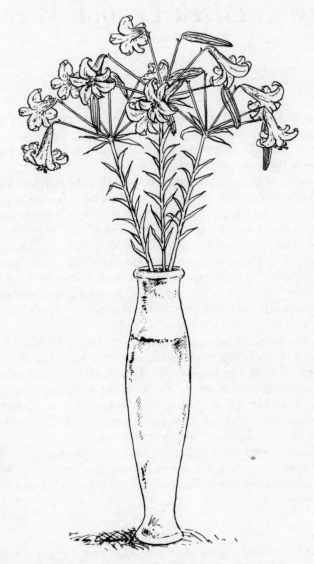

Lilium regale, *your favourite flower, artlessly bunched in a tall vase.*

Pests, Diseases and Weeds

Unfortunately pests, diseases and weeds have no scruples; they will appear in the best gardens.

True avant-gardeners believe that the only way to rid a garden of weeds is thoroughly to clear the soil in the first place by digging it over (sort of agricultural aerobics) and then to pull out by hand any weeds that subsequently push up. Weedkiller is usually resorted to only on gravel paths and drives, and then it's applied with a watering can theatrically marked with a skull and crossbones.

Cheats can use 'Tumbleweed' to clear derelict land, but they risk a resurgence of the problem if they haven't done the job properly, and the wrath of their neighbours if the stuff blows over the hedge.

Once the land is clean it's mulching, mulching all the way, with bark, peat, leafmould, compost and manure. But there's always the hoe if you can't afford the organic blanket.

Pests (the things that move) and diseases (the things that don't) are often tolerated. No avant-gardener ever resorted to anything as organised as a 'spray programme'. Really bad attacks are usually blasted with insecticide or fungicide in the vain hope that they'll quickly disappear. (The avant-gardener knows that prevention is better than cure, but then there never seems to be time to prevent all the beasts and blights from swarming in.)

The selection of chemicals calls for care. Specific aphicides that kill greenfly and yet leave the ladybirds and bees unharmed are chosen whenever possible. But even these are second choice to companion planting.

Apply your 'Tumbleweed' properly, or you may find the weeds springing up again behind you.

Companion planting

In spite of the fact that few of these remedies work, there's a certain kind of satisfaction to be derived from interplanting tagetes with capsicums to repel whitefly; planting pennyroyal to ward off ants; planting chives under your apple trees to keep away scab, and growing nettles among your soft fruit to promote better crops.

The Soil Association, Walnut Tree Manor, Haughley, Stowmarket, Suffolk, has useful booklets that provide details.

Excuses

Where pests, diseases and weeds are overwhelmingly obvious you might like to resort to one of the following:

❧ The butterflies love those nettles.
❧ We keep the greenfly as food for the ladybirds.
❧ Dandelions make such delicious wine.
❧ That's our wild garden.
❧ The girls do so love making daisy chains.
❧ Oxalis is such an effective ground cover plant.
❧ You mean you've never eaten ground elder?

Social Calendar

The avant-gardener's social calendar is very kindly organised by the Royal Horticultural Society, Vincent Square, London SW1. Other gardening events are staged throughout Britain, but none of these is obligatory.

High spot of the year (and the one occasion when your attendance is vital) is Chelsea Flower Show, held in the grounds of the Royal Hospital during the third week in May.

The show runs from Tuesday (Fellows' Day) to Friday. Tuesday is the only day you contemplate going for, like all avant-gardeners, you are a fully paid up member of the RHS. If you happen to know a member of the press you'll do your best to wheedle your way into the show on the Monday, but it's extremely difficult.

A notebook is essential for jotting down the names of plants you intend to introduce to your garden. Do not worry about over-ordering. Any rash decisions can be cancelled by telephone the following week. You would do well to remember the following before embarking on a day at Chelsea:

- There is always a queue for the ladies' loo.
- Pork pies are iniquitously expensive (cheaper to take a Fortnum's hamper and eat your repast on the grass by the bandstand)
- It's quieter before 10 am and after 5 pm.
- It usually rains.
- The marquee now has a one-way system.
- You can buy things shorter than about four feet. Anything longer must be ordered or sawn in half.
- You can chat to personalities of your choice (if you can get near them) – see name dropping on page 12.
- Lay in a packet of Radox for your feet when returning home.

Chelsea Flower Show – high spot of the avant-gardener's year. Photo: Amateur Gardening.

The only other engagements in your calendar are optional visits to the RHS shows at Westminster in the New and Old Halls. It's such a shame that the exhibiting nurserymen can sell plants, though; it makes for such a crush. Still, you continue to support the society even though the subscription keeps going up to cover the repair of the roof over one of the halls (you forget which – they seem to take it in turns).

An annual visit to Wisley keeps you in touch with what's going on (and allows you to see which part of the rock garden is being rebuilt at the moment).

Dress
For the Westminster shows you can wear normal daytime dress. Chelsea should be regarded as similar in standing to Henley, Wimbledon or Royal Ascot (though a large picture hat will not endear you to those standing behind you alongside a floral display or garden). For gentlemen: lounge suits, not morning dress.

Having a Man In

Or a woman; but most likely a man. When you tumble that gardening is actually quite hard work, and when your hands and back decide that they'd be happier given a rest, it's time to take on staff.

There are two basic categories of staff:

❧ Treasures
❧ Tolerables

The Treasures
They will cater for your every whim, thinking ahead and anticipating most of your gardening problems, fads and fancies. They know which plants you love and which you hate. They are quite good at recognising weeds. They are prepared to be flexible about hours and about their duties (they cope with the children and the pets when the occasion demands). They know the difference between weedkiller and insecticide. They work inside when it rains instead of going home. They will bring plants and seeds for you to try. They will listen to your requests and plant things just where you ask. They are capable of making their own cup of coffee. They are tidy. They clean their tools. They are rarer than blue roses.

The Tolerables
They are often inherited. They resent change. Their favourite flowers are chrysanthemums, dahlias, gladioli, scarlet salvias, orange French marigolds, standard fuchsias and lobelia and alyssum. They love 'dot' plants. They have difficulty in recognising your treasures and pull them up as weeds. They insist on a manicured lawn. They will

Tolerable but domineering – your man is likely to impose his own execrable taste on your flower borders.

not allow you into the conservatory during working hours. The vegetables they grow will be their favourites, not yours. They don't hold with new fangled tools/sprays/ideas. They dig beds where you don't want them and act on 'initiative' without asking if you actually wanted the orchard felling. They don't come to work if the weather's bad/their corn is playing up/they put in twenty minutes' overtime last week and you forgot to pay them for it. They don't let you know when they're not coming in (it pays to keep you guessing). They manage to keep their jobs. But then staff are so difficult to find these days.

High Societies

There are around a hundred specialist societies devoted to various aspects of gardening. Fortunately you need not belong to them all.

The Royal Horticultural Society

The one society of which membership is essential to avant-gardeners is the Royal Horticultural Society, Vincent Square, London SW1. For a fee in double figures the Society will allow you to visit flower shows in Westminster, to use the library in Westminster, to visit the Chelsea Flower Show on preview day, and to visit the gardens at Wisley whenever you feel the urge.

FLAWS   You may not live near London. (Not to worry; you'll still receive the monthly journal – see page 112.) Levies are imposed from time to time to mend roofs. Chelsea Flower Show is very crowded (and they'll never move it to Battersea Park).

Northern Horticultural Society

Harlow Car Gardens, Harrogate, North Yorkshire. The Tyke's Wisley. Any avant-gardener within striking distance of Harrogate (such a nice town) should belong. There are specialist groups within the society to cater for specialist interests, and a quarterly journal. There's an annual seed distribution, too.

FLAWS   Lancastrians may object to the garden being situated on the wrong side of the Pennines. Londoners will have a long way to travel.

National Council for the Conservation of Plants and Gardens

The NCCPG is just the society for keen gardeners wishing to make names for themselves. There are lots of local committees set up to check out rare garden plants and undiscovered gardens. Details from

Symbols of High Society membership.

the RHS at Wisley. Be prepared to spend lots of time writing up lists of rare plants. No one seems quite certain what happens to them, but at least it's a job well done.

Of the specialist societies, the following are bound to appeal to avant-gardeners:

GARDEN HISTORY SOCIETY
PO Box 10, Dorking, Surrey.
(For those as interested in gardening books as gardening, and for those whose life's work it is to prepare a four-page pamphlet on a small garden in the Orkneys with a rustic folly built during the Crimean War. The bibliography runs to 12 pages.)

TRADESCANT TRUST
7 The Little Boltons, London SW10.
A society that is setting up a museum of garden history in an old London church. Learn to pronounce the name before you join (tra-*dess*-cant – shades of Cholmondeley there).

THE NATIONAL TRUST
42 Queen Anne's Gate, London SW1.
They buy up old buildings and gardens and make their members pay for them in return for being allowed to look round.

INTERNATIONAL DENDROLOGY SOCIETY
Whistley Green Farmhouse, Hurst, Reading, Berkshire.
Really upmarket tree society that takes its members on tours around foreign gardens with big trees.

The Education of a Gardener

Ideally you learned all you know from your mother. If she left a few gaps and you want to fill them, then take a short course to add status as well as knowledge to your horticultural acumen.

Look no further than:

❀ The Garden School, Godspiece Leaze, Norton St Philip, Bath.
❀ The Inchbald School of Design, 7 Eaton Gate, London SW1.
❀ John Brookes, Clock House, Denmans, Fontwell, Arundel, Sussex.

On the Shelf

Your gardening bookshelf will speak volumes about the way in which you garden. Make sure that all the following authors appear:

Vita Sackville-West (her *Garden Books*).
Christopher Lloyd (the complete works, but with an especially well-thumbed copy of *The Well-Tempered Garden*).
W. J. Bean (the four-part tree and shrub bible at around £160).
Graham Stuart Thomas (complete works but especially his shrub rose books).
Anne Scott-James (her book on *Sissinghurst*).
Robert Gathorne-Hardy (the ones with the Nash illustrations).
A. T. Johnson (the complete works).
Reginald Farrer (*The English Rock Garden*, written in 1919 by this opinionated Yorkshireman).
E. A. Bowles (his *Crocus* and *Narcissus* books).
Arthur Hellyer (anything).
William Robinson (*The English Flower Garden*).
Gertrude Jekyll (anything).
Mrs. C. W. Earle (*Pot Pourri From A Surrey Garden* – even if you live in Wigan).
Alice M. Coats (her horticultural history books).
Russell Page (*The Education of a Gardener*).
W. Keble Martin (the cleric's *British Flora*, beautifully illustrated).
John Raven (*The Botanist's Garden*).
Frances Perry (*Water Gardening*).
Alvilde Lees Milne and Rosemary Verey (*The Englishman's Garden* and *The Englishwoman's Garden*).
Alan Bloom (his perennial plant books).
Joy Larkcom (salad, vegetable and herb books).

Your bookshelf speaks volumes about you.

Beth Chatto (*The Dry Garden* and *The Damp Garden*, even if your garden's neither).
Hillier's Manual of Trees & Shrubs (the pocket bible).
Frederick Stern (*A Chalk Garden*).
Reginald Kaye (*Hardy Ferns*).

Extra marks if the books are signed by the authors. If you really want to lead the field invest in an original copy of Gerald's Herball of 1633. It doesn't need to be signed.

As far as periodicals go, you're happy with the RHS Journal (now known as *The Garden*). Dedicated avant-gardeners subscribe to: *The Plantsman*, 19 Garrick Street, London WC2E 9AX (even though they don't understand half the articles).

Newspaper readers will fall upon:

Christopher Lloyd (*The Observer Magazine*)
Fred Whitsey (*The Daily Telegraph*)
Robert Pearson (*The Sunday Telegraph*)
Arthur Hellyer (*The Financial Times*)

And for a weekly thumb-through take your pick between *Amateur Gardening* and *Popular Gardening*.

Garden Visiting

Each spring you must arm yourself with two little books, one yellow and one green, that will act as your passports to gardens of the rich and famous during the summer. The yellow *Gardens of England & Wales Open to the Public*, and the green *Gardens to Visit* books are packed with plots of majestic or minuscule proportions whose owners are prepared to let the hordes tread their greensward, all in the cause of charity. The yellow book supports the district nurses, and the green book the Gardeners' Royal Benevolent Society.

Garden visiting is an essential pastime for the social climber. Keep your eyes peeled and you may spot the owner, with whom you can have an informed chat on the finer points of some obscure herbaceous perennial, with an eye to name-dropping later.

However, garden visiting can be fraught with peril, and it's as well to be armed with some general information that will help you to interpret the descriptions found within the books. These are always well-intentioned, but sometimes a trifle misleading.

Terminology

Maintained single-handed   Neglected.
Designed by owner   No apparent design at all.
Originally laid out by Capability Brown   Past it.
Created in the past five years   Not yet up to it.
In the process of being restored and replanned   Chaotic.
Planned for year-round colour   Includes a heather garden and a holly bush.
Specialising in rhododendrons   Not worth visiting after May.
Specialising in old roses   Not worth visiting after June.
Famous herbaceous borders   Not worth visiting before July.
Woodland garden   Dense thicket intersected by muddy paths.

Essential handbooks for the social climber.

Woodland walks   Muddy paths.
Pleasant lakeside walk   Bring your wellies.
Wild garden   Bring your machete.
Picnicking in grounds   Bring your groundsheet.
White Garden   Situated close to flour mill.
Parkland   Fields.
Orchard planted with rare varieties   Field with saplings.
Specimen trees   Thinly planted.
Many plants labelled   Many more not labelled.
Refreshments   Stewed tea, bitter coffee, broken biscuits.
Plant stall   A trestle table groaning under the weight of geraniums and spider plants (no sign of the rarities you spotted in the garden).
Dogs welcome   But woe betide you if your wolfhound waters the
    wisteria.

Symbols

Peculiar signs may appear next to the entries in the books. Experience has shown that these indicate the following circumstances:

★ The AA and RAC consider that the catering at this establishment is worth no more than one star.

● Ball games are encouraged on the lawns.

† The local cemetery is handy for victims of catering facilities.

♿ All steps have been replaced with ramps which ensure that wheelchairs are impossible to push uphill. Coming downhill, the pedestrian attached to the handgrips will be lifted smartly off his/her feet.

△ Please bring a luminous triangle with you. It should be erected behind the wheelchair while you make crash repairs.

The Garden Game

As an alternative to 'I Spy', challenge your neighbours to a game of 'Upper Grasses', awarding yourself points for the rank of the owner of each garden you visit. Score points as follows:

Member of the Royal Family – 10
Duke – 8
Earl, Marquis etc. – 5
Hon. Mr. or Mrs. – 1
No title – minus one point (unless famous gardening personality in which case plus three points)

If you manage to speak to the owner, double your score.

Should you have to make an appointment to visit a garden, award yourself 20 points for nerve.

At the end of September all marks are totted up and the loser takes the winner to tea in the cafeteria at Wisley.

The Books
Gardens of England & Wales Open to the Public, available from the National Gardens Scheme, 57 Lower Belgrave Street, London SW1W 0LR.

Gardens to Visit, available from The Gardeners' Sunday Organisation, Mrs. K. Collett, White Witches, 8 Mapstone Close, Glastonbury, Somerset.

Plant Hunting

Package tours to Portugal are not for the avant-garde. Plant hunting holidays are. On these violent little sorties and sojourns you'll find yourself scaling the peaks of Nepal on the back of some emaciated yak, enjoying panoramic vistas over Himalayan summits and doing your best to catch your foot in the stirrup as you plunge headlong towards an apparently bottomless gorge.

The more spartan your trip, the better. Try to visit avant-garde countries like:

- Nepal
- China
- The Hindu Kush
- India
- Korea
- The Azores
- Uzbekhistan
- The Caucasus
- Kashmir
- Sikkim
- Swedish Lapland

Your holiday will cost you between £1,000 and £4,000 (and you'll need a month off work) but then you can gossip about it for years afterwards.

Endeavour to bring plants back with you so that you can point them out to your garden's visitors:

- My bearer found that 8,000 feet up, you know.
- Quaint little treasure; it always reminds me of Charlie Featherstonehaugh. He plunged to his death trying to pick it.
- Of course the colour is much brighter in the Himalayas.

Go on a plant hunting holiday and find yourself scaling the peaks of Nepal on the back of some emaciated yak.

- I think it's pining for its native habitat.
- Even Roy Lancaster isn't quite sure what it is.

Tour operators
The following will fling you further than your average agent:

- Fairways & Swinford, 37 Abbey Road, St. John's Wood, London NW8.
- Raoul Moxley Travel, 76 Elmbourne Road, London SW17.

The Avant-Gardener's Almanac

In common with Old Moore I offer a few predictions to enable you to keep pace with gardening fashion, fads and fancies over the next twenty years.

In ten years' time
A return to informality. Box hedges and privet peacocks are being felled all over the country to make way for natural-looking gardens.

Following on from the Hosta and Hemerocallis Society (founded in the 1980s) the Bergenia and Brunnera Society makes its debut.

The Royal Horticultural Society opens a third hall in London and is granted a flag day to help pay for the three roofs it now has to repair.

A new slug pellet is invented. It contains dehydrated beer and achieves a great saving in yoghurt cartons. The sales of Watney's Light Ale plummet.

Terry Wogan becomes a TV gardener.

In fifteen years' time
The French Marigold Conservation Society is formed to prevent this lovely flower from disappearing from the seed catalogues. It has now been replaced with 42 varieties of agrostemma, thought to be extinct in the 1980s.

All four RHS halls are taken over by the National Trust.

Gardeners countrywide are suffering from attacks by drunk and disorderly thrushes which have been eating paralytic slugs. Chemical companies withdraw the alcoholic pellets.

Best-selling book of the year is Sir Terry Wogan's *Beyond the Compost Heap*, an anthology of letters sent to him by viewers of his top-rating gardening programme.

In twenty years' time

The formal garden makes its comeback. Clipped box hedges, pillars of yew and peacocks of privet are everywhere. Patios are replaced by terraces.

After many years of protests, Chelsea Flower Show moves to Salisbury Plain.

The Actinidia and Arctostaphylos Society folds. Its three members have split up to go their separate ways.

Lord Wogan is elected President of the Royal Horticultural Society.

The Monopolies Commission is called in to investigate why the Royal Horticultural Society now owns every large hall within a fifteen-mile radius of central London.

Glossary of Gardening Terms

Gardening writers regularly get it in the neck for using terminology that no one can understand, so I offer a selection of gardening terms and their meanings to enable any novice to acquit himself with great aplomb at any garden party.

General terms

LAWN   Loosely applied to any flat green area consisting mainly of grass. This is a fallacy. Most British Standard lawns are 25 per cent grass; 25 per cent assorted weeds; 50 per cent moss. Few British lawns are flat.

PATIO   A few stone slabs on which you can sit.

TOWN GARDEN   A patio surrounded by a wall.

ROCKERY   A spoil heap made from earth dug out to make a garden pool. It is studded with lumps of concrete that were once a patio.

WILD GARDEN   A term used by lazy gardeners when referring to a part of their garden that is now out of control and engulfed by our attractive native flora. Favourite 'wild garden' plants include brambles, ground elder, convolvulus, creeping buttercup, couch grass and marestail.

MIXED BORDER   An herbaceous border with tall weeds in it. After three years it becomes a wild garden (q.v.).

RUSTIC   Badly built.

JUDICIOUS PRUNING   No pruning at all.

PUDDLED   1) Slightly soft in the head. 2) The mud around a young cabbage plant which has again been soaked in the belief that the plant is a native of swamps and bogs.

Plant descriptions
Most of these are to be found in seed and plant catalogues:

RUSTIC *Learn from experience to interpret this as 'badly built'.*

GERMINATION MAY BE ERRATIC Don't expect more than one seedling to come up every six months.

GERMINATION MAY BE SLOW Don't expect anything to come up.

EXCELLENT IN BEDS A reflection on the plant's performance in the flower border rather than the divan.

VIBRANT (also **GAY**, **VIVID**) Guaranteed to clash with anything else in the garden.

MUTED Dingy.

F_1 **HYBRID** Big, loud and expensive.

F_2 **HYBRID** Not quite so big, not quite so loud and not quite so expensive.

HYBRID TEA The experts will tell you that this term has now been superseded by 'large-flowered'. Ignore them. You will drink countless cups of this stuff on summer Sundays if you visit local gardens that are open for the day. Both the National Gardens

Scheme yellow book and the Gardeners' Sunday green book (see page 114) are your Egon Ronay guides to hybrid tea.

INTERESTING/UNUSUAL/CURIOUS   Insignificant, bordering on the deadly dull. You'll have a job to spot any flowers.

NEW   Newish.

NOVELTY   Newer than new.

HIGH ALPINE   Guaranteed to die at altitudes lower than 10,000 feet.

SOMEWHAT TENDER   Guaranteed to die at temperatures lower than 23°C.

BONE HARDY   Will come through a cold winter with no ill effects but will probably die in a wet one.

SEEDS FREELY   A pain in the neck.

MILDLY INVASIVE   A pain in the back.

MIFFY   Likely to die because you haven't a clue how to grow it.

NEAT   *A tiny plant that will quickly be swamped by its neighbours.*

SQUINNY   A precursor of 'miffy'; the plant has not yet died but looks as if it soon will.

CHOICE   Used in nursery catalogues so that a high price can be charged for the plant so described.

RARE   As for 'choice'.

NEAT   Quickly swamped by other plants.

NEW FOR 1985   Extinct in 1986.

POTENTILLA 'RED ACE'   An orange potentilla that may turn red on the 21st July if the wind is in the right direction, the rain holds off and the sun doesn't shine.

ROSE 'BLUE MOON'   A rose that has never been blue and never will be but it smells nice.

Vegetable descriptions

The vegetable sections of the seed catalogues can rival estate agents' handouts when it comes to superlatives and euphemisms. Keep a look-out for:

CRISP   Hard as nails.

IMPROVED   Better than the one you thought was best.

ASTRINGENT FLAVOUR   Bitter.

NUTRITIOUS   It doesn't taste nice but at least you know it's doing you good.

SMALL   Minute.

MEDIUM-SIZED   Small.

GIANT   Medium-sized.

BITE-SIZED   Very large.

ESTEEMED FOR BOILING   As tough as old boots if eaten raw.

STANDS WELL   Likely to outlive you unless you uproot it.

UNIFORM HEADS   A description of cabbage. This means that every one of the hundred or so cabbages on your plot will come to maturity on the same day. A must for a family of vegetarian slave labourers who own a dozen chest freezers.

OPEN POLLINATED   The vegetable kingdom's equivalent of a loose woman.

Excuses

Showing visitors around your garden is both a pleasure and a night-mare. It's fun to swank, but supposing they don't like it, or the flowers are just not up to it? Arm yourself with a few suitable excuses, and you and your garden will come through with flags flying:

- You should have been here last week.
- Of course, the weather's been so bad that everything's late this year.
- We rather like it wild.
- It's a terrible year for mildew.
- We've only been here five years and we're really just waiting to see what comes up.
- We lost so much in the winter of 81/82 that we're still getting over it.
- Of course, the drought's ruined the roses/delphiniums/lilies this year.
- One just can't get the staff these days.
- We've been away so much this year that we've just had to let it go.
- Normally they're a picture by now.
- I know there are not many flowers but then I do agree with Graham Thomas that green is the most important colour in the garden; don't you?
- Ground elder is such a pretty plant.